LANGUAGE
OF THE
Soul

WHEN THE SOUL SPEAKS:
THE SIGNS AND SYMBOLS
SPIRIT USES TO HELP US HEAL

LUCIANNE HENRY

BALBOA
PRESS
A DIVISION OF HAY HOUSE

Balboa Press books may be ordered through booksellers or by contacting:

Balboa Press
A Division of Hay House
1663 Liberty Drive
Bloomington, IN 47403
www.balboapress.com
1 (877) 407-4847

Because of the dynamic nature of the Internet, any web addresses or links contained
in this book may have changed since publication and may no longer be valid. The views
expressed in this work are solely those of the author and do not necessarily reflect the
views of the publisher, and the publisher hereby disclaims any responsibility for them.

The author of this book does not dispense medical advice or prescribe the use
of any technique as a form of treatment for physical, emotional, or medical
problems without the advice of a physician, either directly or indirectly. The
intent of the author is only to offer information of a general nature to help you
in your quest for emotional and spiritual well-being. In the event you use any
of the information in this book for yourself, which is your constitutional right,
the author and the publisher assume no responsibility for your actions.

Any people depicted in stock imagery provided by Thinkstock are models,
and such images are being used for illustrative purposes only.
Certain stock imagery © Thinkstock.

Print information available on the last page.

ISBN: 978-1-5043-8068-3 (sc)
ISBN: 978-1-5043-8067-6 (hc)
ISBN: 978-1-5043-8137-6 (e)

Library of Congress Control Number: 2017908173

Balboa Press rev. date: 06/09/2017

Here's What's Inside

Introduction

"There's a voice that doesn't use words, listen"
~Rumi

Time and time again, I've witnessed people feeling distraught following the loss of a loved one, convincing themselves that the sum of whom their loved one once was is in fact the physical body they encompassed while here on earth and that they are now gone forever. My response to that is "really?" Is that all you believe your loved one was, a physical body? What about their thoughts? Their love for you? The way they made you feel? Their personality? Their sense of humour? Their laughter? The words they spoke to you? Their talents? The important lessons they have taught you and the legacy they have imprinted here on earth? Were these things merely hair, skin, bones and organs? Do you really believe that? Of course not. If your loved one was still living here on earth in a comatose vegetative state, would that make your sadness go away? Would you not still long for their "spirit", their "essence", their "energy"? These "things" that we can't seem to measure, the "presence" or "quintessence" of their being is what we miss.

My good friend Angus lived in a non- responsive state for many years. I can assure you that, although I was happy he was still living, I greatly missed the carefree happy soul I once knew. The good news is that this "thing" that we can't define, the "soul" never really dies. It "was" way before it inhabited the physical body it chose to occupy during its time here on Earth and it continues to "be" long after it leaves that body.

Most scientists and physicists agree that nothing on earth is real and that everything is illusion. Quantum physics describes all things as made of particles and energy. Just remember that all things you now use here on earth originated from nothing but a thought. Without a thought it wouldn't exist. Call it God, call it Divine Being, call it the Tao, call it what you will, we all come from the same source. A source that cannot be defined by modern science. We just need to expand our hearts and minds and we will be open to a whole new mystical reality that is available to all of us, if we just tap into it. Your loved one's soul is longing to connect with you. They use their "energy" in a multitude of ways to comfort you and let you know they are ok and happy, if you would just take a moment to notice. This book has been in the works in my heart for many years just yearning to come out. It seems "spirit" just didn't want to let it go and has been knocking on my door consistently, showing me signs and telling me "please explain it to them, so they too can hear".

See on July 25th, 2001, my life changed forever. My fiancé and best friend of 8yrs, tragically passed in a motorcycle accident 6 weeks before our wedding was to take place. On that day, I lost my will to live. My dreams and my hope for the future were gone in the blink of an eye. "What am I to do now?" I would ask myself "where do I go from here?". Well Craig (that was my fiancé's name) wasn't going to let it go. He made sure I felt his presence and he made it known to me whenever I needed it, I just had to "open my eyes".

Since then I have suffered even more losses in my life, my good friend Angus, who passed due to complications of Diabetes and also my grandfather, with whom I was close and also two of my beloved furry friends. They too have made their presence known.

St. Ignatius of Loyola (1491-1556) once said "If God sends you many sufferings it is a sign that he has a great plan for you". My wish for you, is that this book opens your mind to a whole new world and shows you the different ways your loved ones are trying to communicate with you.

I hope it brings you the comfort of knowing that they are right there beside you, all you have to do is let yourself be open to their energy.

From my soul to yours, Namaste

Lucianne Henry

Why People Struggle About Talking About Spirit

I 've always been bewildered by the fact that we all find it easier to talk about spirit when we are going through trying times in our lives. After the death of a loved one or a difficult separation or whatever the situation is, I'll often hear some people say: "This just happened, do you think it's a sign?" Even in an organized church setting, there is much mention of spirit. At funerals we find comfort in saying: "They're now free"or "They're in a better place now". Well, where is this place? And why do we still find it so difficult to talk about it? In our day-to- day lives, the very mention of the word "Spirit" is still very taboo. In fact I was chastised by my own church during the writing of this book by the mere fact that it's about spirit. Something I didn't think was still happening in this day in age. Which is absurd to me, God himself is a spirit we pray to. If we tell other's their loved ones are with God when they pass from this world, does that not mean they're spirit too? If we talk to God and he hears us, do they not hear us too?" It makes me wonder, are we spiritual beings only half of the time? Why is it ok to just talk about in some settings but not others?

That being said, there seems to be a shift in the world towards spiritual awareness and consciousness. However, there's still a lot of work to be done in this area. There are a growing number of spiritual leaders merging the spiritual world into our everyday living. There's a collective awareness taking place. However, what's missing are more platforms for people to be able to discuss the topic of spirituality more freely and openly. I know for me It's always been natural, I have always seen myself and others as a spiritual beings first.

What It Means to Recognize When Spirit Speaks to Us

Recognizing the signs from spirit is like a compass; it helps guide us through our lives. When we are going through struggles in our lives, these are often the times where we are more open to recognizing these cues. I've heard myself and other people say: "Wow, I wonder if that was a sign?" or "I wonder what that meant?" When we can learn to recognize these symbols, it helps us find the comfort we need. It reassures us that we are not alone in this classroom called life. There is confidence in that. Sometimes I'll just ask out there in the ether: "What should I do about this situation?" Especially if it's a situation that I'm struggling with or a decision I'm grappling with. At that exact same time there will be a very clear sign that will come to me, and I'll be like: "Thank you. That's the push I needed to make the decision". Although you can't see them, your loved ones are always around you waiting to guide and help you, but they can't help you if you don't ask,

I believe there are many people in the world feeling lost, without direction. I've seen so many feeling depressed, unsure about their futures, doubting themselves and questioning their next steps.

Even the people who claim to "have faith" have so little confidence in themselves and the Universe around them. If you are one of them, I want you to realize that there is something else out there than what is happening in front of your eyes. I want you to regain confidence in the things that you used to believe in. I want you to reclaim your own power, and regain confidence in your own judgement. If you believe that what you're seeing or hearing is a manifestation from spirit then it is, stop doubting it and start trusting in yourself. After all you are a spiritual being living a human existence and not the other way around. You have a "knowing" inside you that is more powerful than anything else in this physical world. This "internal knowing" was entrusted in you by your creator, whatever you may call him, and it is "all knowing". You have to learn to trust in it.

How to Recognize the Signs and Symbols Spirit Uses to Help Us Heal

Over the years I've identified symbols or signs that spirit uses when trying to communicate with us. There are definitely more, but these are the ones that keep recurring in my life and many of the lives of my loved ones. See if any of these resonate with you.

Synchronicity

"Synchronicity or Coincidence is really divine intelligence
acting upon our thoughts".
~*James Van Praagh*

I call the first type of sign synchronicity. This can also be called serendipity, just like the 2001 movie with John Cusack and Kate Beckinsale. Another word for synchronicity is coincidence. But I don't believe in coincidences. I believe there are only synchronistic events. I believe every encounter in our lives is predestined and happens to teach us something. For example, a lot of times I'll be thinking of someone I haven't thought about in a while—and I know this happens to a lot of people—and that person ends up calling me or I'll run into them, even if it's been a long time since I've seen them or heard from them. I've also heard stories where for some reason a person is running late or they take a different route and they find out later that there's been an accident on the street they usually take. I suspect it wasn't a coincidence at all that they ended up taking a different route. I believe that a spiritual intervention took place and they were meant to avoid that accident

Often times when we notice a synchronicity, a lot of us will brush it off and say: "Oh, wow, that was a coincidence!" I think that where we get empowered is when we recognize and affirm that there is an actual force out there that we can't explain. That maybe it isn't a coincidence, maybe we are being spiritually guided. That's where we find our power. It's in the comfort of knowing that we're not alone. We are always being guided and we need to learn to recognize it.

My friend Sylvie shared this account with me: "In 2012, we found a lump on my breast. From there I had to go for a Mammogram then a biopsy. The toughest part for me was waiting for the results. It took about a month from the time we found the lump to my appointment for my results. You can imagine the emotions that goes threw your mind. So when the day finally came to find out, I was sitting in the waiting room with Ray my fiancé, when a man came and sat right in front of us. There were very few people in this large waiting room but this man chose to sit right in front of us. If I didn't know any better, I would have thought it was my Dad. My Dad died of emphysema, so for a long time he had trouble breathing. And the way he would breathe and position himself was the exact same way this man was breathing. I was in shock. I took out my phone and texted Ray who was right next to me because the man was that close I didn't want to talk out loud. I said to him... OMG BABE, I think my Dad is here. He looked at me a bit confused then I looked at the man. He knew exactly what I meant even if he had never met my Dad. The man didn't have my dad's looks but his breathing, posture, body type... I could of closed my eyes and swear it was him. That's when I knew.... I had Cancer. I was going to get really bad news but I was going to be ok. It was my dad's way of letting me know he was with me and I was going to be OK. Just then, the nurses called me in the office. My hunch proved correct, I had Cancer. But I wasn't scared, I felt my dad's presence that day and I somehow knew I was going to be ok. I've been Cancer free for 5 years now."

Let me share with you a personal experience that happened after Craig, my fiancé, passed. The weeks following his funeral I stayed with my parents. My mom was convinced I was moving back home. But I decided I needed to face life head on so I decided to return to the home Craig and I used to share. One of the first mornings I woke up in the apartment was probably one of the lowest moments in my life. I felt very depressed and alone. At that very moment, the telephone rang. It was a good friend of mine. She asked me to go for breakfast. Not only was the idea of her calling me to go for breakfast or calling me at all very out of the ordinary for her, but I've come to realize that it was an intervention from somewhere else, somewhere that I can't explain. I instinctively knew that her call that morning wasn't a coincidence. In some way she saved me that morning.

Here's another story to help illustrate this point. One week before Craig's passing, the pastor who was set to officiate at our wedding called us. He told us that he was being transferred to another church and he wouldn't be able to officiate at our wedding. He gave us the name of the new pastor that would be performing our wedding ceremony. He told us that we would hear from this new pastor in the next few weeks to set up an appointment to meet with us. As fate would have it, that call never came.

The morning of Craig's accident, I was sitting in the hospital chapel praying that he would survive the accident. A nurse came in and asked me If I wanted a chaplain to come pray with me. I agreed and the chaplain walked in and introduced himself. When he said his name I nearly fainted. He was the "new" Pastor who was to officiate at our wedding. He sat down next to me and said "You know, I never do chaplaincy at this hospital, but they called me this morning because they were stuck and really needed someone." Was it a coincidence that they called this particular Pastor? I'll let you decide. But immediately I knew it was Craig's way of saying goodbye to me. I realized at that moment that he wasn't going to survive the accident. In fact, just a few minutes later the surgeons walked into the chapel to tell me he wasn't going to make it. I didn't need the doctors' confirmation... I already knew.

As odd as this may sound to you, this "Coincidence" actually brought me comfort because I knew there was a higher power in all of this, more than I could ever understand. Being more aware of where there may be synchronicities in your life will help you realize that you are not alone on this plane we call Earth. By being aware of how spirit works, you will hopefully be able to understand that these fateful occurrences have always been at work in your life, you just needed to be more open to them.

Four days prior to Craig's accident, we were enjoying a family BBQ at my aunt and uncle's cottage. As we were just sitting down to eat, we heard a vey loud crashing sound on the water and people screaming. Two boats had collided together on the river. Craig, my brother-in-law and my cousin's boyfriend had run down in the river to help. Later that night, I found out that instinctively, Craig had jumped in the water and had given CPR to one of the injured people floating in the water. He had never had to give anyone CPR before and was profoundly affected by it. The person ended up passing. He didn't sleep well that night or the following three nights and on the fourth day his own faithful day came. The ironic thing is, his burial site is right beside one of the people who passed in that boating accident, whom he tried to help.

Towards that end, here's another example of synchronicity. Craig always aspired to be a firefighter. Becoming a firefighter was what he wanted the most in his heart of hearts. Sometime after his passing, a mutual friend of ours, who is a firefighter, invited me to a gathering. This is where I met my present husband, who you guessed it…. happens to be a firefighter. I remember the next day calling my mother to tell her I had met someone and that he was a firefighter. She became emotional and, under her breath said: "Craig sent you your firefighter." That really touched me because my mom is not an openly spiritual person. I knew that our meeting was not "by chance". But for my mother to recognize it was very special to me.

I must add that I have a special connection to that particular friend who introduced me to my present husband. He came to me in tears 6 months after Craig's passing and needed to talk to me. As mentioned previously, he's a firefighter. As a first responder, he wanted to tell me that he was the first on the scene at Craig's motorcycle accident on that faithful day. He told me that at the accident, he held Craig's head in his lap to stabilize it until the ambulance arrived. Since Craig was wearing a helmet, he did not realize it was his friend's head he was holding until the next morning when he read his obituary. The fact that he did not recognize his own friend that day affected him deeply. However, I was happy he was there with Craig during these last waking minutes of his life. I told him that if he had known, maybe he wouldn't have been able to do his job to the best of his ability that day. He told me that at the very time he was reading the obituary the next day while sitting in his car, two doves landed on the hood of his car in front of him. Surely a sign from Craig thanking him for helping him and reassuring him. I couldn't think of a better person introducing me to my present husband. Coincidence? I doubt it.

Speaking of Coincidences…or as I call them synchronicities, here's another one for you. I was always afraid of Craig's motorcycle. Not because I thought he was an irresponsible driver, but just the sheer number of motorcycle accidents alone are staggering. I was often on his case about getting rid of the bike, especially since our wedding was coming and we needed the money to help pay for it. On the day of his accident, I learned that Craig was actually on his way to the motorcycle shop to put the motorcycle up for sale. He never made it. He told his brother that morning that he was going to surprise me that evening and tell me he got rid of the motorcycle. Do you see the web of events or synchronicities that kept unfolding during this tragic time in my life?

Rainbows

Rainbows are the most common sign from spirit reported by individuals, especially immediately following the death of a loved one. Rainbows represent Divinity, good luck and oneness. Their arch shape symbolizes "The Gateway to Heaven". The evening we received friends, family and loved ones for visitation during Craig's Funeral, many people attending reported to me that there was a rainbow appearing what seemed to be directly above the Funeral Home. I remember it bringing me such solace during that difficult time. I don't have an intelligent explanation of how spirit materializes a rainbow for their loved ones. Nonetheless, I had a strong "knowing" that he somehow made it happen that evening.

In September 2015, a Memorial was held in Florida for one of my greatest teachers, Dr. Wayne Dyer. There were many reports of a rainbow arching above the convention centre, where the memorial was held that evening. Dr. Dyer was such a ray of hope for many during his life here on Earth, it would only be fitting that he would make his presence known in such a beautiful way on that special evening.

I've had numerous friends tell me they feel Rainbows signify a special connection to their loved ones.

Music and Voices

*"The soul has been given its own ears to hear things that
the mind does not understand"*
~Rumi

I'm sure this has happened to you as it happens to a multitude
of people. You'll get in your car and a song will start playing
on the radio and you think: "I was just thinking of that song." Or
you'll be thinking of someone, and then a song will come on that
reminds you of that person. Maybe it's "your" song or it's a song that
was playing at the time that you were creating memories together. I
believe music is a medium used by spirit to communicate with us.

In the weeks following Craig's accident, there was a song that I
just couldn't get away from. Everywhere I went: if I got in my car,
if I turned the radio on in my home, if I was in a public place the
song *Stuck in a Moment*, by U2 played everywhere. It happened so
much so that at one point I looked up the lyrics to the song because
I felt someone was trying to tell me something. For me, that was
definitely a sign from spirit. They were the perfectly encouraging
words I needed at exactly the right time in my life. Here are just a
few paragraphs of that song so you can judge for yourself:

I never thought you were a fool
But darling look at you
You've got stand up straight carry your own weight
These tears are going nowhere baby

You've got to get yourself together
You've got stuck in a moment
and now you can't get out of it

Not long ago, I met this sweet lady who recently lost her husband of many years. We had a long heartfelt conversation and she shared with me personal occurrences that had been happening since his passing. She was a religious lady and had not shared any of these with anyone out of fear of judgment. Having had my share of judgment since the release of my book from my own church and some family members, I identified with her more than she knew....

Her stories were beautiful...such exquisite testaments to the love they once shared and continue to share. One of the accounts that touched me the most is...this lady and her husband had been taking dance lessons for some time prior to his death. Since his passing she often hears music playing but there are no stereos or radios playing in the home when she hears it. She has come to recognize the songs she faintly hears. They are the melodies her and her husband used to dance to. Although she questioned and doubted herself at first, as most of us do during these occurrences, she now finds the music comforting and knows her husband is still with her. Is there anything more beautiful?

Sometimes it's not just music we hear....My friend Kathy shared this graceful story with me: " My father was proud, modest, quiet, and a man of few words. I loved my father dearly. Dad was in his mid 40s when he and my mother adopted me. We were a poor family but made do with what we had. I spent most of my time in the barn, helping with the farm animals, planting the gardens, on the tractor working and playing outside with my dad. I left school before grade 11, married young and had a son. I always felt I disappointed my parents. Five years after we married, my husband and I purchased our first home. My father always said to my mom that I would always come back to the farmhouse. He was right. By the time my father was in his late 60s, he began doing subtle but strange things around the house. Unbeknownst to us, he was beginning to show signs of Alzheimer's. By the time he was in his 70s, he was diagnosed with the disease and we moved back home to help my mom. My father spend the last 6 months of his life in a nursing home. He never really knew me as an adult, the successful job I had landed or the great life I had built for myself and my family. The week before he passed, the nursing home, where he resided, was closed due to a contagious virus. When it re-opened, I was scheduled to visit with my father on a Monday evening. But as I approached the nursing home, something made me drive by. I decided I would go on Tuesday instead with my mother. That night as when I went to bed, I was almost asleep, when I heard the words: "I know you made it". I opened my eyes and sat up in the bed, this was my father's voice as clear as day. At 10:00am the next morning, I received a call from the nursing home staff suggesting that I should come. At the time I did not know my mother and a family friend were already there in my father's room . Nor did

I know mom was holding my father's hand and told him I had arrived, as she had seen me parking my vehicle. My father took his last breaths a few steps before I made it to his bedroom door. I spent a few minutes alone with my father that morning and thanked him for his words the night before. I felt calm about his passing, Although I knew my father loved me, I never heard him say the words. However, the night before, the words whispered in my ear by his spirit, reinforced his love for me".

Media/Electronic Devices

"The sound waves are vibrations,…it's the ability to
adjust your senses so you can feel the music"
~ David Mason

Along with music, another way spirit communicates with us
is by manipulating media. I don't pretend to know how this
happens. However, media is energy and everything on this earth
including human beings are energy, so it would make sense. An
example of this was with the use of a recordable device. I had
bought Craig a recordable keychain because he was very forgetful.
Every time I asked him to get something at the store on his way
home, he would often forget or come home with the wrong thing.
So, as a joke, I got him a recordable keychain. I recorded a cute
little message on it which said, "Love you, honey." It was hanging on
the key rack in our apartment. On one of the more difficult nights
following my return to our apartment, I was sitting there feeling
extremely alone and I heard the words: "Love you, honey." I looked
around and thought I was losing my mind literally, then it clicked,
it was the keychain! It was playing on its own!

I've recounted this story to a few people. The most popular

response I received was: "Oh, it was probably the batteries in the keychain that were going dead". But I never really accepted that explanation because how could batteries going dead make something automatically play? For an object to play, it needs the energy from the batteries. By going dead, the batteries would do the opposite, it would prevent it from working, not spontaneously play. I didn't need confirmation from anyone that what I heard was real. I knew in my heart they were the comforting words that I needed at that exact time to snap me out of my sadness.

As little at they may be, animals spirits can also manipulate electronic devices. My beloved little Pomeranian Pepi passed one morning a few years ago in my arms from heart failure. When I returned home from the Veterinarian's office I picked up the phone to call my mom to share the news with her and to my dismay, I couldn't get a dial tone just a static noise. I thought that was funny since it had never happened before. I kept trying too call her and finally after one hour, I was able to get a dial tone. Later that same morning, when my husband learned about Pepi's passing, he came home from work. When he walked in the kitchen, he noticed that the range hood light was out. He remarked on how he had left that light on because he sensed that Pepi wasn't feeling well that morning as it was dark in the house. The odd thing was he had just changed the light bulb in the range hood the week prior. I knew it was Pepi's small way of saying thank you for the leaving the light on and that he was still with us.

I was very close to my grandfather. One of his greatest passions was astronomy. As a child I pretended to be interested in astronomy just so I could spend one-on-one time with him. We would go stargazing at night and he would show me constellations, stars and planets, and I pretended I knew what he was talking about.

It ended up being this endearing connection we shared, astronomy became "our thing"! My grandfather passed 5 years ago, the same year my daughter Maya was born. One day recently, I was thinking about him more than usual. I got in my car that morning and the song *A Sky Full of Stars*, by Coldplay started playing. Of course, initially I thought: "That's just a coincidence," and I laughed it off. Later on, as I returned home, my daughter was watching the cartoon *Caillou*, and "falling stars" was the theme of that cartoon episode that day. Then I started thinking: "Hmm, that seems a little strange." I was laughing about the reference to stars. Then finally that same night, as I was watching TV, I looked out the living room window and saw a falling star. At that point, I knew these weren't merely coincidences. I knew they were signs from my grandfather. His spirit was clearly trying to connect with me that day.

It filled my heart that he had attempted to connect with me because my grandfather was a very technical person and rarely spoke of spirituality. Except for one day a few months before his passing when he had a bad fall in the kitchen when no one was home. He said that he must have blacked out for a few minutes because he "saw a beautiful bright light where he was free from pain". He said: "if that is what heaven is like, I can't wait to go". Two days prior to his death he also told his daytime Caretaker that he was awoken in the night and when he turned around there were two men dressed in robes standing at his bedroom doorway with a bright light behind them. When his Caretaker learned of his passing, she called my mother to tell her what he shared with her a few days prior. It brought my mom, and the family, great comfort in knowing he was in a higher place.

Butterflies

"What the caterpillar calls the end of the world, the
Master calls a butterfly"
~ Richard Bach

Butterflies are definitely a sign to look for. White butterflies have been a recurring symbol for me. In the weeks following Craig's death, up to this day, white butterflies follow me everywhere. It doesn't matter where I am, they just seemed to appear. I've come to accept them as a token from him that he's watching over me and that I'm not alone in this sometimes confusing human existence.

"my white butterfly"

Butterflies represent the shedding of an earthbound shell giving birth to a weightless being with wings. Much of what the human physical form goes through when its spirit sheds its physical vessel. I think that's why butterflies are such a strong symbol for connecting with a loved one once they've left this physical plane.

One of my good friends Line has butterflies visit all Summer. She instinctively knows it is a sign from her maternal grandmother. Last spring she recounted that the butterfly came early with another one in tow...her uncle had passed away the night before and she only found out later that he had passed. This same grandmother, she feels, is whom she attributes the birth of her gorgeous daughter to. After years of trying to conceive, she had finally given up hope, she was, in her words: "too tired and heartbroken". Two weeks after her grandmother passed, she was pregnant with her daughter. She knows in her heart this was not a coincidence and that her grandmother played a part in this miracle. She used to pray to her and ask for her help. She says she's come to accept it as just the way it is now. She doesn't get nervous when these things occur in her life, she just smiles and nods towards the sky.

My step mother-in-law shared he following beautiful story with me: "The butterfly has appeared in my life many times in the past few years. Each time has been very meaningful as I realized my mother's spirit was visiting me. My mom had poor health for several years before she passed on and she spent most her time quietly resting. Her summers were spent on a swing in the backyard and often our conversations were of the birds, the butterflies she observed throughout the summer afternoons.

After she was gone and especially around the anniversary of her passing, thinking of her and missing her, a butterfly would appear and I would know it was her visiting me. Each time I would be comforted and feel her presence so strongly.

We spent summers by the ocean and my mom would relax in the lounge watching us in the water or on the beach. This past summer we returned to the ocean and I was alone with my two young granddaughters having a wonderful afternoon. My mom had loved spending time with my girls her granddaughters. While walking along the path to the beach, there was a beautiful butterfly that followed us. I know it was my mom's spirit and I felt a joy, the joy of her being there and of knowing her spirit now was free to soar.

In the week leading up to the anniversary of her passing this year I found myself missing her very much. Butterflies began appearing everyday, each time I was comforted and knew she was with me. One evening I knew I was to go to a place and there I found a beautiful canvas with a large butterfly on it. I brought it home and placed it on the mantle, later that night I felt my mother's spirit in the room with me and now each time I look at the canvas I know she is always here".

I can't reiterate enough how when these signs occur in our lives, our souls instinctively know they are from spirit. It's the feeling they leave us with that marks us the most.

Butterflies have always had a special meaning to my friend Diane. She believes they are a sign from her father. On a rainy day after her father's passing she was waiting in the car for her son. She noticed a beautiful butterfly flying around him as he walked towards the car. She also noticed her son had stopped to look at the butterfly as it continued to fly circles around him then it finally landed on the hood of car. Under her breath Diane said: "Hi dad, I know it's you". As her son opened the door of the car and sat down he said to her: "Pépère came to visit us". Pépère is the french term for grandfather. How wonderful that her son recognized the butterfly as a sign of his grandfather too.

Birds

"In order to see birds, it is necessary to be part of the silence"
~ *Robert Lynch*

B utterflies are not the only common sign of spirit but so are birds. While I do have a special connection with Eagles as you will hear later on in this book, I've also learned from listening to others share their stories about how they connect with spirit. Last year, my good friend's father passed away. After the funeral, his family and friends were all gathered on the back patio of the family home. A hummingbird kept insistently flying around us, it just wouldn't go away. We all thought it was endearing how this hummingbird was just flying around us. My friend's mother then said: "That hummingbird's been around here for days and just won't leave. I'm pretty sure it's Albert". It all brought a small tear to our eyes. I loved that she recognized it because I was already thinking it. I think it brought my friend's mom comfort to know that maybe her husband was letting her know in his own special way that his spirit was still around.

Insects/Flowers

*"Everything is determined by forces over which we have
no control. It is determined for the insects, as well as for
the stars, human beings, vegetables or cosmic dust. We
all dance to a mysterious tune, intoned in the distance by
an invisible piper"*
~Albert Einstein

I t has been said that the name "Lady Bug" originates from the name "the Beetle of Our Lady" stemming from farmers in the Middle Ages praying to the Virgin Mary to save their crops. Swarms of ladybugs were sent, ate up all the pests and saved the crops. From that point on Ladybugs have been deemed a sign of Divine energy and protection.

I have resided in three different homes since Craig's passing. In each home, regardless of the season, I can find ladybugs all around my home. I have asked many friends and family if they have a similar "pest" issue. To the best of my knowledge, very few have experienced the same. Here is a photo of a ladybug sitting on the back of my chair just recently. May I remind you it was the middle of Winter at the time of this photo on a cold blistery day.

my ladybug

Apart from the spiritual meaning of the word Ladybug as mentioned previously; where it gets personal for me is the fact that the very first pet Craig and I owned together was a guinea pig named "Lady". Craig was very much an animal lover and he adored that little thing. He was devastated when she passed just a few short years prior to his own passing. The morning he found her he called me at work crying asking me to come home. I feel in my heart that these "Lady" bugs are Craig's cute way of telling me "Lady" is with him.

Dragonflies are another very popular sign from spirit. Dragonflies are a sign of survival. Since the time of the dinosaurs, dragonflies have stayed virtually unchanged. My friend Diane's husband feels his father's spirit comes through as a dragonfly. On a particular Fall day, about one year after his father's passing, her husband was longing for his father. He was searching for a sign from his father that day. Since it was Fall, he remarked to Diane, that he doubted he would get his sign because dragonflies aren't usually around in the Fall. As they entered a store shortly after, a song, that was popular during the time of his father's passing, was playing. Every time he hears this song it reminds him of his dad. He got particularly emotional so he decided to go wait in the car. Diane continued in the store and looked for her son who had been wandering around in the store. When she caught up to him, something caught he eye on the wall...a picture of a dragonfly. She immediately called her husband from her cell phone to tell him what he had just seen. Although it wasn't the real dragonfly her husband had been looking for, the symbolism of the dragonfly picture and the song playing at the same time, defies the odds of a coincidence. They just knew it was from him.

One Spring Day while visiting her grandmother's grave, my friend Claire noticed that these little white flowers were growing only in front of the grave and nowhere else in the cemetery. She told her father about it and he explained that they are called "May flowers" and that they were her grandmother's favourite flower. Her father too has since passed and guess what now grows uniquely in front of his headstone....what a special display of affection.

actual photo of May flowers taken by my friend

I should mention that this past Winter, when speaking to Claire she excitingly described to me that in front of her father's headstone, formed in the snow, was a perfect little rectangle of ice. She thought to herself: "It almost looks like a miniature hockey rink".

Later that day, she was speaking to her brother and she told him that she had stopped by their father's grave. He says to her: "Did you see the little hockey rink". Their father was an avid hockey fan and they both had the exact same thought and feeling when they saw that little ice rink. You know it's a sign, when it leaves not only you with a lasting impression but also other friends or family members around you.

Coins and Feathers

"He will cover you with his feathers, he will shelter you
with his wings"
~ Psalm 91:4

Feathers have long been known to signify Spirit presence is around us. Native Canadians and Americans believe feathers signify honour and are connected to the Creator. During the writing of this book, I often prayed and asked for guidance. Recently, I went through yet another difficult time in my life. My husband and I had been trying to conceive for quite some time. I was nearly three months pregnant and sadly lost the baby. As I was leaving the Hospital that day and got in my car, on the passenger seat was a beautiful white feather. Here is the actual photo of the feather:

white feather

Spirit never ceases to amaze me. If I am open to it and I ask for guidance it almost always reveals itself to me. I knew I wasn't alone that day and that everything was going to be ok. The "Angels" were with me that day...my little tiny "Angel". In the midst of my loss, I trusted that there was a higher power in control. It was an event I do think was synchronistic. For this to happen during the writing of this book was not a coincidence. Maybe someone reading this book needed to hear about what I went through so they also could heal. The lesson to be learned here is don't be afraid to ask for guidance. Spirit is always waiting to comfort you and reveal itself to you... if you just remain open to it and trust it.

Coins are another type of symbol to look for. I don't have any personal experience with coins but I know many people feel coins are a sign from their loved ones. Many times coins, especially pennies, will be placed in your path or in unusual places. Here on Earth money is energy, it is traded for just about anything you can think of. Therefore, it makes sense that spirit would use them as a symbol of their energy. Pennies are the most common. It is said that they signify "oneness" because their value is "one" cent.

Unlike myself, my sister doesn't often speak about spirit. I guess you could say it makes her uncomfortable. However, during the writing of this book, a string of events began to occur in her life. One night after she had gone to bed, she noticed the living room light was shining in her bedroom. She remarked to her partner Mike: "I thought we turned the living room light off".…."we did" he replied…There was nobody else in the house, or was there? They began speaking of signs from loved ones and he recounted to my sister how a friend of his finds coins randomly everywhere. This friend is convinced they are a sign from her father. And there began a strange unfolding of events. My sister got up to go to the washroom that same night and she found a dime on the floor. She had just gone to bed a few minutes prior and walked in that exact spot, she never noticed the dime.

The next day, my sister met our mother for coffee. While ordering her coffee, she was telling my mother about the occurrences of the night before, as the cashier handed her the change….five dimes! And that wasn't it for the dimes….A few days later, working her post as a Nurse, one of her patient's family had gathered around the patient as he was taking his last breaths. Emotionally charged, my sister stepped out of the room to catch her breath. She sat at the the Nurse's Station to refocus for a minute and when she looked up…yup wouldn't you believe it…a dime! It impacted her so much that she sent me this photo:

actual photo at Nurse's desk taken by my sister

My sister attributed the dimes to our grandfather. My sister and our grandfather shared a special bond. She had been feeling especially stressed in the weeks leading up to the occurrences and she felt that he was letting her know that he was by her side. That's the thing about signs from spirit, it's the "feeling" they impress upon you, a certain knowing they leave you with. And they seem to happen at just the right time.

And that's not the end of her episode with the dimes...the day following her shift at the Hospital, my sister ran into our grandfather's caretaker, who she hadn't seen since his passing. That just confirmed to her what she already suspected about the dimes. She heard our grandfather loud and clear.

My good friend Line's grandfather passed during the writing of this book. It was just around the same time as my sister's encounter with the dimes so I shared the stories with my friend. The next day, Line sent me a message to tell me that as she was ordering a coffee at the same coffee shop as my sister, and there it was, a dime on the floor in front of her! Later that day she was at the local Shopping Mall and in her pathway, as she was walking, was a stack of coins, neatly stacked in the middle of the floor. What were the chances? Near to none I would say. I told her that her grandfather must have been listening to our conversation on the day of his passing and he was trying to let her know he was ok. What a beautiful unfolding of synchronicites. They keep confirming to me how close to us our loved ones still are.

My friend Diane, that I spoke of earlier in the book, shared that not only does her father-in- law communicate with them through dragonflies and music but also dimes. Her husband had been shopping for a truck and needed to make a decision about it. When he opened the door there was a dime on the floor. He wondered if that was his dad helping him with his decision. After he actually purchased the truck, he had to bring it to a garage to get fixed. There, stuck to the driver's side window was another dime. This brings comfort to her husband that his father is still there with him, helping him through the events in his life.

The following anecdote has nothing to do with coins or feathers but it demonstrates how Spirit is always guiding you. A few years ago, my husband and I decided it was time to sell our home. We were successful in selling our home. However, the only problem is the home we were going to buy was no longer available. I was quite stressed about the situation. We no longer had just ourselves to worry about in life but it was our responsibility to provide a home for our daughter. One day I just gave it to God and said: "You always know best; I'll leave it in your hands". That same day I was at a store and spotted a print that for some reason caught my eye. I just couldn't leave it there. I had to buy it; something was telling me to.

Shortly thereafter, we did end up finding a home. One that I must add was already sold when it was shown to us. As fate would have it, the offer fell through on the home the day following our visit. We ended up immediately writing an offer and here I am sitting writing this book as I am looking out at the view outside my window. I can't show you my print because of copyright laws but as I'm sitting here looking at the view outside my window, it looks eerily similar to the view on the print. Now I know why I was attracted to that print. I was being guided by spirit that day.

the view outside my window

Scents

*"Nothing is more memorable than a smell. One scent can
be unexpected, momentary, and fleeting, yet conjure up a
childhood Summer beside a lake in the mountains".*
~Diane Ackerman

Following the passing of a loved one, it is a common occurrence to notice the scent of their perfume or a scent that reminds you of them. It is NOT your imagination and what you smell IS real. The week following Craig's death when I was still staying with my parents, I distinctively smelled his perfume one morning while standing in the kitchen. My ego was trying to tell me it was my imagination but my instinct knew it was undoubtedly Craig's cologne.

It's not just the smell of his cologne. The month following Craig's passing I spent hours upon hours just sitting outdoors. Mostly spent on a park bench listening to the birds singing and breathing in the fresh air. It's about all I could bring myself to do. Sometimes, when I am sitting outdoors in the Summertime, especially when he crosses my mind, a familiar smell will take me right back to my days on that park bench. The familiar smells embrace me and console me.

My beloved grandfather, lived in my parental home during the last years of his life. My daughter Maya has now claimed his room when we visit my parents and calls it "her" room. Sometimes when I lie there at night reading Maya a bedtime story, I can smell my grandfather's cologne. I know his Spirit is with us and that he sees the amazing young girl Maya is becoming.

Animal Instinct

"The eternal being, as it lives in us, also lives in every animal"
~Arthur Schopenhauer".

Animal instinct is another form of energy that can't be explained. The more I study animals, the more I recognize there's another force in charge that is not human. Animals have a sixth sense about them that we humans also have, but social conditioning has taught us not to trust it. Animals can sense danger before it happens. There are many reports of animals running away and seeking refuge long before natural disasters such as earthquakes, tornadoes and tsunamis hit. Some working dogs can sense seizures in humans minutes before they occur and signal their owners that it's coming preventing serious falls. Other dogs can sense low or high blood sugars in diabetics and alert their owners preventing injuries. I think as humans we are conditioned to not trust this gut instinct. We let our thoughts take over and we believe if something can't be explained then it must not be real.

I recently read a story of the elephants of Thula Thula. A conservationist by the name Lawrence Anthony worked with rogue elephants for many years and saved many elephants' lives.

They called him the *Elephant Whisperer*. His family reported the story of two separate herds of wild elephants in a single file making a 12-hour trip to the family compound in the days following his passing. The elephants sat there quietly at the family compound, they didn't eat or drink, for two whole days. After the two days, they made the 12-hour trek back to their habitat. The family was in such awe and so touched that they took a photo of the elephants.

That story is remarkable to me. How did these elephants know this man had passed? They wanted to pay their respect to the man who had helped saved them. For them to know his spirit had left his body and to make their way to his family compound 12 hours away is an illustration of a power that defies our understanding. For a link to actual photo of the elephants of Thula Thula making their way to the Anthony compound visit my website referenced at the end of this book.

I believe since animals are so instinctive and can sense spirit, they are used by spirit to communicate with us. Craig and I had two pet bunnies: Fuzzy and Gizmo. The first Christmas after his passing, his parents had come to spend Christmas with my family. After the Christmas Eve service, we had decided that we all wanted to visit his gravesite. This was behind our family church where we attended the service, so we all got in the same car.

There was a little path where you could actually drive down to the gravesite. There was freshly fallen snow on the ground. My father was driving the car that night and he remarked: "Look at that. There are bunny tracks leading directly to the headstone." There are times in life when no words are needed, this was one of them. We were all thinking the same thing: we were all thinking that was a sign from Craig, to let us know that he was okay and that his soul was with us. It was a deeply touching experience for us.

I don't pretend to know how these things happen, but one thing I know for sure is that we certainly all felt it that night. Kind of like the magic you feel at Christmastime, you can't see it but you definitely sense it. We seem to notice these occurrences more after tragic events. I believe it's because we are more open to them as we are closest to our true self during these trying times. But then our day-to-day lives and social conditioning seem to harden us and lead us to dismiss all that we can't explain.

Just last year, my four legged best friend Winston, a greyhound we adopted through a rescue organization lost his battle with lymphoma. After leaving the vet's office, on our way home, a bald eagle flew in very close vicinity to our car. It was an unusual place to see a bald eagle because it was close to the city centre. It brought me such comfort because it represented freedom to me. It was a symbol that Winston was finally free: free from his lymphoma and free from the confines of the racetrack where he spent many years. Ever since that time, I see bald eagles just about everywhere. I feel that he is still with me. I think this illustrates that not only can human spirits manipulate certain things to let us know that they're okay, but I also think that animal energy can do the same. I'm not saying the eagle was Winston. I'm not saying he's the bird. But in some mysterious way I think that spirit has a way of making these things happen.

Shortly after Winston passed I also started noticing what looked like the image of the face of dog on the ceramic tile flooring downstairs where he spent most of his time. Maya, our five-year-old daughter can see it too. We had been in our home for just over a year when Winston passed but I never noticed the image before. Funny how we notice these "signs" when our spirit and hearts are more open. Can you make out the dog's face?

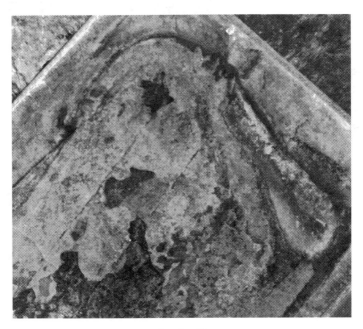

dog in tile

Numbers

*"The breeze at dawn has something to tell you, don't go
back to sleep"*
~ *Rumi*

When it comes to spirit energy, numbers are very interesting. I've been reading a lot of literature on this topic. For many people, including myself, certain numbers are very meaningful in our lives and keep recurring. For example, it's a common occurrence for people to wake up at the same time every night. For me, it's 3:13am. I look at my alarm clock and I'm awake at that exact time many times throughout the week. I didn't know why this was happening, so I started reading up on it. There's a lot of documentation supporting the fact that many individuals wake up between 3:00 and 4:00am Some spiritual authors have suggested that this is a time when we are the most in tune with our souls and that spirit is trying to communicate with us. If you too wake at the same time in the early morning hours, I encourage you to write down your thoughts. You may be surprised at what guidance spirit is trying to offer you in your slumber.

Some numbers or dates, by some unseen force, keep recurring in our lives. For me, the number 25 is very significant. My first date with Craig was on June 25th, we were engaged on December 25th, we had a wedding shower on June 25th, and he passed away on July 25th. For some reason this number keeps repeating itself in my life. In fact, during the writing of this book, another personal event, which I have shared with you, had the number 25 attached to it. Our baby's due date was June 25. I had a bad "gut" feeling about it from the beginning because of it. My doctor thought I was overreacting but my instinct proved correct.

I don't think numbers and dates are just happenstance. I believe some occurrences in our lives are predestined and numbers and dates are used to confirm to us that they were meant to happen. These numbers are "anchors" or "markers" so to speak. They don't have to be just attached to negative events. Sometimes they can also be linked to positive events. Either way, it's a way for spirit to let you know your life it on track, these dates are essentially your "life markers".

Another recurring number in my life is 1111. It isn't unique to me, this recurring number is a common one for many. Numerologists believe that 1111 is a number that appears more often than any other number. It appears more often than can be explained by chance or coincidence. Some believe that the number 1111 signals a spirit presence. At least four to five times a week I look at the clock at 1:11 or 11:11. Does this happen to you? Now I just smile when it occurs knowing that spiritual guidance is around me.

Recently, I had to make a very important career choice that I was struggling with. I had to make the decision to attend an important training session in a different city. On a whim, I decided to go. When I got to my hotel room that evening, to my amazement my hotel room number was... drumroll please...1111! That evening when I saw that number on my door, it affected me so much that I took a photo. I felt like I was being guided, like I had made the right decision.

"actual photo of my hotel room door"

Shortly following her father's passing, my friend Claire shared with me that she began seeing the 1:11 or 11:11 nominations very frequently everywhere. The days following our conversations, funny enough I began seeing the number combination more frequently that usual. I think someone was listening to our conversation that evening and was trying to confirm what we already knew!

A few months ago I attended a session by a medium in my hometown. For those of you who are wondering, yes I do believe in mediums. Nothing on this planet is solid. Everything including humans are made up of energy: particles moving at a high speed of vibration. I don't believe Heaven is a place in the clouds as depicted on photos since the dawn of the ages. I've flown through the clouds in an airplane and I know Heaven is not there. Heaven is just another plane of existence moving at an extremely high speed of vibration that I believe some people have been given the special gift to feel or sense.

I was really looking forward to the session that evening. There were a few loved ones I was hoping would come through for me that evening. At the end of the session, I was really disappointed because I didn't really feel like I got a clear message from anyone. But all through the event that night, the medium kept looking my way and saying that she had been seeing the number three everywhere all day. She said she felt like it was coming from my direction, like it was meant for me. However, the number three didn't mean anything to me. Although, the next morning it occurred to me that my good friend Angus, who passed away from complications of diabetes, was into car racing. I thought maybe the number three had to do with a race car. I'm not familiar with car racing, so I contacted his mom. She told me the number three was very significant because one of Angus's favourite drivers, was Dale Earnhardt Sr. She said he actually met Dale Earnhardt Sr.'s wife while on tour at a racing museum a few years prior. She reminded me that he had number three memorabilia everywhere in his basement. I remembered he had car memorabilia, but I didn't recall the number three. That is a perfect example of how I almost missed an attempt by spirit trying to communicate with me. I was so quick to dismiss the experience. As it turns out the number three was extremely meaningful.

My friend Diane was especially thinking of her father one day. She was reading on a social media site an article about signs of afterlife. One of the signs mentioned were numbers reflecting the date of someone's passing. One of the very next posts on the site after she read this had a photo of an alarm clock in the background. The time on the alarm clock was 3:17. Not a common time really. But it meant something for her...her father passed on March 17th. See how signs are very subtle at times and very easy to miss? Spirit tries hard to communicate with us but we often discard the signs or are too distracted to notice. I need to mention.... This same friend, who's father passed suddenly on March 17th? This date also happens to be her father-in-law's birthday. Who I should mention, also passed suddenly five weeks later. Coincidence? Well, I'm sure you know how I feel about coincidences at this point.

Clouds and Heart Formations

"Clouds come floating into my life, no longer to carry
rain or usher storms, but to add colour to my sunset sky".
~ Rabindranath Tagore

While we're on the topic of symbols, another illustration occurred during the writing of this book. You see this book has been in the works for a long time for me. It's been on my "bucket list"; something that I've been wanting to do for a long time. One evening on my drive home, I was weighing the decision to publish the book asking myself if this was the right thing for me to do at this juncture in my life. I looked up at the sky in front of me and there seemed to be what looked like a cross in the sky. It was the push I needed. At that point I knew I was making the right decision. I was so moved that I stopped the car on the side of the road and took a photo.

"+o\111 po.on of fle aoss in the skY'

Spirit was really working hard that evening. On the same night, I brought home Chinese food for supper. After we were done eating I opened my fortune cookie and on it read: "Every action of yours inspires others." I don't remember having ever received that fortune before. At that point, there was no doubt in my mind that publishing this book was part of my destiny.

"actual photo of fortune cookie"

Some people have reported, following the death of a loved one, finding heart formations on objects or object themselves being shaped like a heart. Although it has been 16 yrs since his passing, Craig still reminds me that he is watching over me and my family. Even after 16 yrs, I still find the day of the anniversary of his death difficult. The sights, the smells, etc, just bring the memories right back and I find the day very difficult. On the morning of this past anniversary of his death, I was standing in the driveway watching my daughter ride her bike.

As I looked down, on the asphalt was a puddle of water shaped perfectly like a heart. I knew it was from him and it lifted up my spirits knowing he is still around watching over us.

"Heart in the Driveway"

Past Lives

"I seemed to have loved you, in numberless forms,
numberless times, in life after life, in age after age,
forever"
~Rabindranath Tagore

I n the recent years, I've become increasingly fascinated by the subject of past lives. In fact, so much so, that I began researching and studying the subject intensively. We use the saying: "He or she is an old soul" a lot in our culture, which leads me to believe I am not the only one who believes in past lives. Many of my friends feel they're children are old souls. Two of my good friends (and I'm sure they are more) have shared with me that at a very young age (age of 3 or 4), their daughters both sperately expressed to them how happy they were they chose them to be their moms. What do think a child that young could possibly mean by saying "choose"?

Do you have a fascination or interest in things from a certain time passed or era and not really sure why? Or travelled to a new city or country and it felt so familiar to you that you feel like you have been there before? You leave that place and you have such a longing to go back?

A deep sadness when leaving? I'm particularly attracted to things from the late 19th and early 20th centuries. For some reason, I just feel like I lived during this time before. I've always been fascinated with old houses and antiques for as long as I can remember.

There's a popular tourist attraction in my hometown called Kings Landing. where you can actually walk through and visit historic homes dating from the early 1700s to the early 1900s. The furniture is reflective of these eras and they even have actors walking around in costume. Every time I visit that place I feel a certain nostalgia: it feels familiar and even smells familiar. I even feel sad when it's time to leave, like I'm leaving my home behind. Why would I feel this way? I theorize that I must have lived during this time before.

There are numerous accounts of children around the world spontaneously blurting out glimpses of their past lives to their parents. Many parents have reported their children saying things like: "My other mommy had curly hair" or: "You're much nicer than my other daddy" or even: "I miss my other home". See *Memories of Heaven by Wayne Dyer and Dee Games (2015)*. I recently came across three stories that peaked my interest in past lives. These accounts defy logic.

The first involves the story of Anne Frank, who lost her life in a concentration camp in 1945. Less than ten years later, in 1954, a girl by the name of Barbro Karlen was born in Sweden. When Barbro was just 3-years-old, she adamantly did not like her parents calling her Barbro. She insisted they call her Anne Frank. Her parents thought it was really strange that their little girl would be asking them to call her Anne. They didn't even know who Anne Frank was. Barbro kept having these recurrences or unfounded fears. She was afraid of men in uniform. She was terrified of having a shower, and she wanted nothing to do with eating beans. Barbro's parents began researching Anne Frank's story. It then made sense to them why Barbro was so terrified of taking a shower or men in uniform because Anne Frank died in a concentration camp during the Holocaust. Anne Frank also wrote in her diary that she lived on beans for two years while hiding in her parent's attic. That also explained Barbro's repulsion to beans.

When Barbro was ten, her parents decided to visit Anne Frank's childhood home in Amsterdam. It had been turned into a museum. Although the family had never been to Amsterdam, they didn't need a map because Barbro led them directly to the house. This is a 10-yr-old girl in a strange city of a population of about 800,000, and she guided her parents exactly to the house. She immediately ran up the stairs and started feeling the wall and asked, "Where did my movie star pictures go?" The museum tour guide present that day was dumbfounded. They had just taken down the original movie star posters that Anne Frank had on the wall to have them framed. How would this young girl know the directions to this house, and know about these posters? When Barbro arrived at the house, she even commented on how differently it looked. This story defies conscious reasoning but she somehow had been there before. What's even more shocking is the actual physical resemblance between Anne Frank and Barbro Karlen.

Here's a similar story. A little boy named James Leininger was born in 1998. When he was just 2-yrs-old, he would have terrifying nightmares. In the middle of the night, he would scream things like, "Airplane crash! Plane on fire! Little man can't get out!" When his mother would ask him questions about his dreams, he would know amazing details like the name of the plane that he was flying, he said it was a "Corsair". He said things like: "Big Red Sun. Japanese shot him down." He would draw graphic pictures of airplane battle, and he would sign his name "James 3". James didn't even know how to spell yet at that point. To his parents' amazement, when watching World War II documentaries, 3-year-old James would correct the narrator on the types of planes and bombs used in battle. He even knew the name of the airplane carrier his plane took off from: the *US Natoma*.

His parents had a difficult time accepting the possibility that James could have lived a past life as it conflicted with their strong Christians beliefs. But the accuracy of the information their 3-yr-old boy would blurt out was astonishing. James' parents started doing a lot of research on the subject. They discovered that there was in fact an American aircraft carrier that actually had gone down in World War II battle, and the name of the pilot was James Houston Jr. (Remember this little boy would sign his name "James 3"). James Houston Jr had died 50 years before the little boy was born. James' mom started asking him if there were other people that he knew or if he had friends in his previous life. James said there was another pilot that was also involved in the plane crash by the name of Jack Larson. During their research, they uncovered that there was actually another plane that had crashed around the same time and the name of the pilot was in fact Jack Larson. Just as Barbro Karlen, the physical similarities between James Leininger and James Houston are remarkable. For a link to view photos of Barbro Karlen/Anne Frank and James Leininger/James Houston visit my website mentioned at the end of this book.

The third story involves Eli Lasch MD, a prominent physician in Israel who investigated a reincarnation case in which a 3-year-old boy remembered a past lifetime in which he was murdered with an axe. From what the little boy told his parents and the physician, it was believed that the boy used to live in a nearby village. The parents brought the boy to visit two nearby villages before finding the third village that he says was very familiar to him. The boy recognized his prior home and led them directly to the man who murdered him. He walked up directly to his murderer, named the man by name and told him: "I used to be your neighbour. We had a fight and you killed me with an axe". The boy led them directly to where his body had been buried. The villagers recalled a man going missing 4 years prior. The murderer was astounded and confessed to the killing. Inexplicably, the 3-yr-old boy had a red birth mark where he says he was hit with the axe.

Dreams

"In a dream, in a vision of the night, while slumbering on their beds, then He opens the ears of men, and seals their instruction."
~Book of Job (33: 15-16)

Sometimes we accuse our dreams of not making sense, but I think that dreams offer us a lot of information on our lives. During our sleep is when our subconscious mind is in full swing. There are some experts who believe that we can actually travel between spirit and earthly dimensions during our sleep. It's called astral travel. There are also a lot of accounts of people seeing their past loved ones in dreams. A lot of times we'll just say: "It doesn't make sense". But I firmly believe that they can visit us in dreams and that we shouldn't discount it even if the dream itself doesn't make sense.

My beautiful friend Tracey, shared this story with me: "After my brother passed away in December of 1994, I was broken. He had been my best friend and what I believe to be my souls mate ever since the day we first met. In fact, he was the one who named me Tracey. You see my mother had chosen the name Leanne. But when my brother saw me he was adamant that I was indeed a Tracey! (His favorite tv show at the time was The Trouble with Tracey). We went through life very much as a duo

When he fell ill to Aids in the early 90s our lives changed forever. We became closer than ever. I would often fly to Toronto, where he lived, to be with him. We would talk of Angels often and the afterlife. I asked him if it were possible that he would visit me from Heaven to let me know he was OK. He did just that many times in my dreams after he crossed over. Messages were clear and he always showed me his freedom and peace in many different dreams but I still ached for his human presence. I grieved so deeply I thought I might die at times.

On this one particular night I laid in bed with tears running down my face, my soul screaming out to him. Where are you? I would say or How could you leave me here all alone? That's when a warmth came over my entire body and as I looked into the nights sky I saw a shooting star. Then another and then another. I had to rub my eyes as I had been crying so hard but the stars kept shooting. What was I seeing? My tears turned to laughter as I saw at least 50 shooting stars flying across the night's sky that night. Then I heard a voice saying: I never left you and I never will. I have not cried one tear for him since that night".

Another friend of mine disclosed that following her father's passing, she often wondered if he was ok. He suffered from Schizophrenia and wasn't coherent at the time of his passing. She also had many regrets about not spending time with his during the years leading up to his death. She remembers vividly him visiting in a dream. He held her in his arms and told her he was free for any pain. He told her he loved her and not to have any regrets. She woke up crying hysterically. Again, it's the feeling it these visitations and signs leave you with. And I have no doubt they are visitations. There are no such things as dreams just manifestations of feelings and visitations. Visitations that leave us so touched, we never forget them.

I've had my own manifestations during my slumber. One night I awoke from my sleep and I clearly saw this short little old lady standing beside my dresser not far from my bed. I did not feel threatened at all as she seemed very sweet and gentle. She had shoulder length grey hair. She was wearing glasses, a dress and an apron. Then she disappeared. The next morning, I was quick to dismiss it as a dream but I do recall seeing her very distinctly. I told my mother about my dream and she said that the description of the little old lady matched that of her grandmother's. She said that her grandmother wore glasses and always wore an apron. The funny thing is, the dresser she was standing beside in my vision once belonged to my great-grandmother. My mom had handed the dresser down to me. This is a good place to add that Spirit will commonly make their energy known near or through belongings they once owned.

Recently I was walking through an old house and I felt a presence there with me, like I wasn't alone. At that exact moment my husband called me to ask me if I had ever spoken to our daughter Maya about Craig. Maya is 5-yrs-old so I've been waiting for her to be a little older before explaining anything to her yet about him. "Well" my husband said, "she just said to me, you know Mommy was married before". As I hung up the telephone, I looked up and there on a door was engraved the letter "C". Here is an actual photo of the door.

the door with the 'C'

About a month after Craig passed, I had a dream that I was in this beautiful Romanesque temple. I can't even begin to explain to you how beautiful it was. It had large tall columns, and it was just the most beautiful place I had ever seen! Walking towards me was Craig, but he was dressed in Egyptian or Roman garb, a skirt and tall boots. Of course, as I awoke, my logical mind told me that this dream didn't make any sense. But it was him as clear as day, and I remember feeling such comfort from that dream, I was so happy to see him. In this dream, beside me to my right, there was a short column. Sitting on the column was a book. The pages of the book were flipping, and each page contained scenes or flashes from my life. I woke up from this dream feeling such a strong rush of emotions. It was by far the most memorable dream I have ever had!

Fast forward 10 years, my husband and I were on a cruise ship and I was reading a book by Sylvia Browne called *Life on the Other Side*. In the book, she depicts this place where we first go when we leave this earth. She first describes a tunnel. After this tunnel we come to a big Romanesque building that she calls *The Hall of Wisdom*. Her description of the *Hall of Wisdom* is the exact depiction of the place that I visited in my dream 10 years earlier. She describes the exact tall pillars and what she calls a "scanning machine" that goes through the scenes of our lives. I just couldn't believe what I was reading, I was in shock! I felt so excited that I ran around the cruise boat trying to track down my husband to tell him about what I read and to tell him about my dream. I had never told anyone about my dream. He totally thought I was losing my mind!

I know what I experienced that night wasn't just a dream I do believe in astral travel and that in our slumber our souls sometimes catch a glimpse of the spiritual plane. I visited a place that night that was other than here on earth. The following photo is an image similar to the Hall of Wisdom I vividly remember from my dream (although it was much more incredibly beautiful in my dream)

Hall of Wisdom

Near Death Experiences (NDE)

*"My Soul is from elsewhere, I'm sure of that, and I
intend to end up there"*
~Rumi

There are a few near-death experiences I have read about in the recent years that I can't ignore. There's a significant lesson to be learned from these encounters. I think they are proof that there is a spirit world out there, and that there is a lot more to our existence here on Earth than we care to admit. A story that I read recently was about a lady by the name of Anita Moorjani. She's a bestselling author of a book called *Dying To Be Me*. In 2006, after battling lymphoma for four years, she was admitted to the hospital. Her organs had shut down and she was given only hours to live. She had slipped into a coma and her family had gathered all around her for her final hours.

As she recalls in her book, *Dying To Be Me*, during this comatose stage she remembers crossing over to the other side and seeing her friend who had also passed from cancer years before. Her father who had also crossed over was also there to greet her. She remembers vivid details of her near-death experience. She heard everything that was said in her hospital room during that time. She remembers hearing her husband and family members crying. She recalls coming back into her body following the advice of her friend and father. They told her she needed to come back because she had unfinished business and things she had yet to accomplish before her time here on Earth was over. Anita did come back to her cancer- ravaged body. Three days later, something miraculous happened there was almost no trace of cancer. Months later, she was totally cancer-free. The medical world has no explanation for Anita's recovery. Sometimes we want to explain things in physical terms, but I think it's very empowering for us to know that we actually have control over our health if we just believe in our own light. Anita underlines in her book that in Heaven "there is only love".

Another great example of an NDE is the story of a four-year-old boy named Colton Burpo. In 2014, a movie based on his story, *Heaven Is For Real,* was released. Colton had undergone emergency surgery for a ruptured appendix when he crossed over to the other side. In the months following his surgery, the four-year-old had vivid memories of what he saw in Heaven; details that a little four-year-old boy could not possibly know. He remembered seeing his mom praying in the hospital room and his dad screaming at God for letting this happen to his son. These were private moments only his parents knew about. He also told his parents that he met his grandfather and sister while in Heaven. The boy meeting his sister was especially touching for his parents who had miscarried before Colton was born. They had never disclosed this to him.

Colton's father, a Wesleyan Pastor, had a difficult time accepting that his son had a NDE. However, after such detailed accounts of Heaven from such a young boy, he could no longer discount his son's memories.

The third story is that of 9-year-old Annabel Beam, who has been turned into the 2016 best-selling movie *Miracles from Heaven*. After four and a half years of a chronic, progressive and incurable illness, Annabel had stopped fighting. One day Annabel fell 30 feet into a hollow tree and emerged physically unscathed, cured of the 'incurable' illness that had plagued her and claimed to have gone to heaven where she sat on "Jesus' lap". To read more on these stories, please visit my website and follow the links.

Children

*"Grown men can learn from very little children, for their
hearts are pure. Therefore, the Great Spirit may show
them many things which the older people miss"*
~Black Elk

I think we should pay more attention to children and listen closely to what they have to say. Their souls are still fresh from Heaven and unsullied by social expectations. I think that we have a lot to learn from them. There are many accounts of children saying strange things that parents unfortunately brush off as "silly". My daughter Maya was only 3 months old when my grandfather passed. At 18 months, she inexplicably could pick him out from a photo as if he was familiar to her.

On another occasion, when Maya was four we were on our way to her dance lesson when I had just learned of her favourite dance instructor's passing. I was anxious about how I was going to deliver the news to her. That evening, I was tying her dance shoes when she pointed to something behind me. She said: "There's Madame." Madame is the name she used for her dance teacher. I looked back and all I saw behind me was a wall. Thinking maybe I misunderstood, I asked her to repeat what she said, and again she answered with a look of excitement on her face: "There's Madame!" It was very clear to her that she had seen Madame. And nothing was ever said again about it. I later tried asking her questions like what Madame looked like, but she couldn't understand why I insisted on asking her questions about it. To her, it was like any other dance lesson and she didn't want to discuss it anymore. I had chills in the back of my neck the rest of that evening. But deep down I knew what she saw was real to her.

I have a few friends of mine who's children, at very young ages, have expressed to them how happy they were they picked them as parents. Now, most of us would dismiss that as silly children talk. However, why do you think children would say such a thing, if they didn't exist as souls prior to their journey here?

There is a child prodigy by the name of Akiane Kramarik. This little girl was just four when she started painting incredibly detailed images of Jesus. She says that "God speaks to her" and that she receives these images from "Heaven". At the age of eight she painted the face of Jesus entitled the *Prince of Peace*. This piece has such remarkable detail that it's difficult to believe that it was painted by an 8-yr-old with no formal training. What's more unbelievable is that the name of God had never even been mentioned in her home, as her parents were Atheists. I encourage you to refer to my website for a link to view Akiane's piece entitled *Prince of Peace*.

Orbs

*"The Spirit is never at rest, but always engaged in
progressive motion, giving itself new form"*
~Georg Wilhelm Friedrich Hegel

I n recent years, I've increasingly been noticing Orbs appearing
in families', friends' or my own photos. Orbs are sphere-like
opaque shapes appearing in different colours and sizes. Sometimes
they appear in a group or individually with or without a trail
displaying motion. It is believed that the orb is energy being
transferred from a source (i.e. power lines, heat energy, batteries,
people, etc.) to the spirit so they can manifest. Many skeptics
explain orbs as photography mishaps or specs of dust. However,
most often many shots are taken with the same camera at the same
moment and many times only one shot out of many will show an
orb. If they are just mishaps, why do they not appear in all the
frames taken with the same camera?

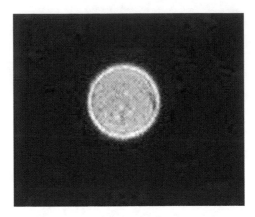

photo of orb

There's a growing interest in orbs *see ORBS: Their Mission & Messages of Hope by Klaus Heinemann PhD and Gundi Heinemann (2010).* Many believe just like microorganisms were unknown to the world before it was discovered with the use of the microscope by Antonie van Leeuwenhoek, one day the veil will be lifted and the Orb will reveal a whole new dimension unknown to us.

A very sweet lady, who has become a dear friend of mine, who lost her son at the age of 18, has several hundred shots spanning the course of many years, of orbs in her photos. She has come to accept them as her sons presence.

I urge you to look through your family photos and find orbs similar to the one above that you may have missed. Your loved one may have been trying to make their energy known to you.

I conclude my labor of love by offering you the following photo. It does not have the usual anatomy of an orb. However, it brought me such joy I wanted to share it with you. I was taking a photo of a sunset one evening and this orb-like shape appeared in the shot. Can you see the smiley face emoji? He even has a halo! I saw it clearly and it made me smile. I hope it makes you smile too.

photo of sunset with emoji

"Stop the words now, open the doors to the center of your heart and let the spirits fly in and out"
~ Rumi

In Memory of

Craig Theriault

Bibliography

Books

Browne, Sylvia & Harrison, Lindsay. *Life on the Other Side.* NAL, 2002.

Dyer, Wayne. *Wishes Fulfilled: Manifesting the Art of Manifesting.* Hay House, 2012.

Dyer, Wayne & Games, Dee. *Memories of Heaven: Children's Astounding Recollections of the Time Before They Came to Earth.* Hay House, 2015.

Heinemann, Klaus & Heinemann, Gundi. *ORBS: Their Mission & Messages of Hope.* Hay House, 2010.

Moorjani, Anita. *Dying To Be Me. My Journey from Cancer, to Near Death, to True Healing.* Hay House, 2014.

Websites

Institute for the Integration of Science, Intuition and Spirit: **www. IISIS.net**

www.Akiane.com www.HeavenLive.org

www.MiraclesFromHeaven-Movie.com

About the Author

Trained in Psychology, Counselling and Reiki, Lucianne has worked in related fields for most of her career. One of her greatest interest has been the pursuit spiritual awareness and personal development. She has been fortunate to travel to many places around the world to be trained by some of the best spiritual and motivational leaders such as Bob Proctor, Chris Widener, Michael Losier, Wayne Dyer, and more. Lucianne receives tremendous joy hearing from others who are also on a journey of spiritual consciousness. Lucianne presently lives in Fredericton with her husband Andrew, their beautiful young daughter Maya, new baby Paige and their furry four legged friends Joey and Daisy.

My greatest wish for you...

We live in a society that has lost most, if not all, of its mysticism, dreams, and hopes. We have turned them into criticism, cynicism, and loss of hope. However, there is a shift taking place, a realization that we are more than our physical bodies. Jesus himself, in the book of John 6:63 said, "It is the Spirit that gives life, the flesh counts for nothing". Yet many of us are so attached to our physical world. There's a non- physical law that guides us and moves us. This law, this synchronicity, as one of my greatest teachers, Dr. Wayne Dyer would say, "is continuously moving the pieces around while we think we are in control."

Although I had to expose many vulnerabilities in the writing of this book, it was worth every word if it helps even just one person who is presently struggling. You may be thinking how is she so blessed to have all these signs occur in her life? I'm not, they are also all around you, if you just take the time to notice them. My wish for you is for you to recognize your greatness as an eternal spirit and to reclaim your power by tapping into this mysterious force that is guiding and moving us all. Learn to recognize this energy that is all around you, and use it to pursue the life of your dreams; the life you were intended to live during your brief physical incarnation here on earth.

To help you continue to live a soulful life and to assist you in continuing to manifest your power and energy, you can join a community of individuals who are also on the same path by:

Option 1: Visiting my website:
www.LanguageoftheSoulBook.com.

Option 2: For other personal stories of Language of the Soul from around the world, conversations and Daily Soul Food, follow me on Facebook: www.facebook.com/ AuthorLucianneHenry. I would love to hear about your own personal experience of how spirit communicates with you.

Notes

S igns and symbols spirit uses to communicate with me...

_____

_____

_____

_____

_____

_____

_____

_____

Lucianne Henry

_____

_____

_____

_____

_____

_____

_____

_____

_____

_____

_____

_____

_____

_____

_____

_____

_____

_____

_____

_____

_____

_____

_____

_____

_____

_____

_____

_____

_____

_____

Lucianne Henry

_____

_____

_____

_____

_____

_____

_____

_____

_____

_____

_____

_____

_____

_____

_____

Lucianne Henry

Lucianne Henry

_____

_____

_____

_____

_____

_____

_____

_____

_____

_____

_____

_____

_____

_____

_____

Lucianne Henry

_____

_____

_____

_____

_____

_____

_____

_____

_____

_____

_____

_____

_____

_____

_____

_____

Printed in the United States
By Bookmasters